TESTAMENT
THE ANIMATED BIBLE
Ruth

TESTAMENT

THE ANIMATED BIBLE

Ruth

STORIES FROM THE OLD TESTAMENT

Adapted by Sally Humble-Jackson

B⊞XTREE   S4C

First published 1997 by Boxtree
an imprint of Macmillan Publishers Ltd
25 Eccleston Place, London, SW1W 9NF
and Basingstoke

Associated companies throughout the world

ISBN 0 7522 1008 4

The publishers would like to thank Derek Hayes of Cartŵn Cymru
for the series title and Eliza Trimby for developing the logo illustration.

A CIP catalogue entry for this book is available from the British Library.

Designed by Clare Truscott
Printed and bound in Italy

Testament: Ruth by Sally Humble-Jackson
(adapted from a script by Penelope Middelboe and Martin Lamb)

Testament: the Animated Bible is a multinational venture conceived by S4C (Channel Four Wales). Produced in Russia, Wales and England, the series has been financed by S4C and the BBC (UK), and Christmas Films (Russia). *Testament* has the endorsement of the Bible Society.

Animation director for 'Ruth':
Galena Beda of Christmas Films, Moscow
Photography by Alexander Vikhansky

Series Editors:
Martin Lamb and Penelope Middelboe,
Right Angle, Tenby, Wales

Producers:
Naomi Jones (Cartŵn Cymru)
Elizabeth Babakhina (Christmas Films)

Associate Producers (BBC):
John Geraint
Geoffrey Marshall-Taylor

Series Executive Producer:
Christopher Grace (S4C)

RUTH

N aomi was crying. The tears ran down her face and into her mouth. They tasted of salt and sadness.

Her two grown-up sons were dead. They had been brought to their father's grave, a small cave in a rocky hillside, and laid tenderly beside him on the ground. Now Naomi knelt in the cave, saying her last goodbye. A small lamp glowed softly, allowing her to see her sons for the last time.

Even though they were wrapped in white linen, she could recognize them. Their features were as familiar to her as the palms of her own hands.

She remembered seeing them for the first time when they had just been born. They had blinked at the light. They had waved their little hands in the air, reaching out for their mother as all new babies do. She had loved them so much, and had gone on loving them just as much as they grew into men. She could not bear to think of them dead, lying forever beside their father in this grave.

Naomi would have crumpled to the floor had it not been for the two brave young women whose arms came around her to support her.

'I'm sorry,' she sobbed. 'I should be comforting you, not the other way round. You're young. You've both lost your husbands…. You loved them so…. And now you're left with nothing.'

Ruth and Orpah comforted their mother-in-law, Naomi.

One of them, Ruth, stroked Naomi's brow. 'But you've had so many troubles to face,' she said. 'It's not long since your own husband, Elimelech, died…. Just when you thought everything was getting better at last.'

Naomi nodded sadly. 'Elimelech was so pleased that we had settled down well here in Moab. He hated taking us from Bethlehem to a foreign country, but what choice did he have? It didn't rain. All the crops stopped growing, the soil on our land turned to dust. We were starving – everyone in Bethlehem was starving. Everyone in the whole of Judea! We had to find somewhere where there was food.' She put her hands to her face and pressed her eyes to stop the tears. 'Maybe it would have been better if we'd stayed in our own country and starved.'

'Don't say that,' whispered Ruth. 'You brought our husbands to Moab. We wouldn't have met them if you hadn't come here.'

Orpah took Naomi's hand. 'We loved your sons just as we love you.'

Naomi smiled. 'May the Lord God bless you. My sons couldn't have chosen better wives.'

When a great stone had been rolled across the mouth of the cave, closing the grave for ever, Naomi gazed out over the plains of Moab. Then she turned her eyes up to the vast evening sky and the red melting sun. She imagined the people of Judea, her own people, gazing up at that same sun. All that divided the two countries was the Great Salt Sea. She had walked around that sea to get here, and she would walk around it again to get back home.

'I must return to Bethlehem,' she said.

The young women were shocked. 'But why, Naomi?'

'God's hand is against me,' she sighed. 'Our family name has ended here in Moab.'

Naomi and Ruth left Moab together.

Ruth and Orpah understood her pain. Naomi's people believed that family names were important. If Naomi had only had a grandson then the name would have lived on.

'We're coming with you,' said Ruth.

Naomi shook her head but Orpah protested. 'It's far too dangerous for a woman to go alone!'

'But what more can I suffer?' Naomi cried. 'I've already lost everything!'

'You still have us,' Ruth reminded her.

Naomi blinked back fresh tears. How she would love to keep them with her – but she had to put their well-being first. 'You must stay here with your own people,' she insisted. 'You're still young, you can marry again.'

The young women knew that if they went with Naomi they would never find new husbands. Moab and Judea were often at war, and anyway, the Judeans expected a widow to marry the nearest male in the family, usually the brother of her dead husband.

'I have no more sons to offer you,' Naomi said sadly.

Orpah bit her lip. Life would be very empty without a child. Men tended their fields and women tended their children.... That was how life had been since the beginning of time. She could not imagine living forever without a husband, without a child. Hard as it was to leave her dear mother-in-law, Orpah felt there was no choice. She would stay in Moab and find a new husband. 'We'll never forget you,' she promised Naomi. 'Never.' Tears stung her eyes as she turned her back and walked away.

But Ruth could not bring herself to go. What if Naomi came to harm on the journey back? What if there was still famine in Judea? Ruth could not let her mother-in-law face the future alone.

'Follow your sister, Ruth,' Naomi urged. 'Go back to your mother.'

'No!' Ruth's eyes burned with love. 'You are my mother now! Where you go, I will go, and where you live, I will live. Your people will be my people and your God my God. Where you die, I will die, and there I will be buried.'

Naomi was stunned by the loyalty in Ruth's words – and the love in her eyes. She did not argue further.

Day after day, the two women trudged across the wilderness towards Bethlehem. To their relief the famine was over, the drought had ended. Judea was lush and green again and the people were well fed. And when the two women stepped through the gates of Bethlehem, women clustered around Naomi, shouting greetings, asking questions.

'Where's your husband? Your sons?'

'Can the earth give up its dead?' Naomi replied heavily.

The women were appalled. 'God have mercy,' one gasped. 'All dead?'

Naomi and Ruth entered the gates of Bethlehem and the women of the town clustered around them.

'Speak of sorrow, not mercy,' Naomi muttered. 'Because God has dealt so bitterly with me.' She took Ruth's hand. 'She is all I have now. Ruth. Wife of my eldest son.'

The women stared uneasily at Ruth. She looked different from them, darker-skinned, as Moabites were. They thought her very strange. Ruth felt embarrassed. She did not know what to say.

But then a little boy came dancing up to them, waving a stick. He hurtled into Ruth who put out a hand to steady him. He looked up at her and smiled sweetly. Ruth bent down and stroked his head. Children were the same the world over – they did not care about people's differences, only their kindnesses. A lump rose in Ruth's throat. She had dreamed of having a little boy of her own one day, a little boy just like this one…. But it would not happen now, would it?

Naomi grieved to see the stricken look in Ruth's eyes. She understood how much Ruth had given up by coming with her.

When Naomi and Ruth reached Naomi's old house, they

saw that it had become dirty and broken-down after being empty for so long. Naomi's friends and neighbours were shocked that the two women planned to live there, but Ruth took her mother-in-law's arm. 'This is my home too,' she said with dignity. 'I live wherever Naomi lives now.'

They had a roof over their heads but the rooms were cold and bare and they had nothing except the clothes they stood up in. The food they had brought with them from Moab was almost gone. The nearby fields, however, were golden with barley. The spring harvest had already begun.

At dawn on their first morning in Bethlehem, Naomi gave her last crust of bread to Ruth. She felt ashamed that she had nothing else to offer the girl who had given up so much to stay with her.

'I'm going to the fields to glean,' Ruth announced.

Naomi was shocked. Only very poor people gleaned, crawling behind the harvesters, scrabbling in the dirt for any stray ears of corn which fell to the ground. 'Scavenging with the poor,' she protested. 'Oh, my child….'

'We are poor,' Ruth said wryly.

Naomi gave Ruth her last crust of bread.

'But the men who are harvesting...' Naomi pulled a face. Oh dear. The men would not treat Ruth with respect once they saw she was a foreigner. 'They could take advantage of you,' she warned.

Ruth knew Naomi was right, but she would not show that she was afraid. 'I'll be careful,' she assured Naomi.

'You're such a stubborn child,' Naomi scolded lovingly. 'A child should listen to her mother!'

'A daughter should work so her mother can eat,' Ruth teased in return.

'Perhaps....' Naomi gave Ruth a hug. 'May the Lord God keep you safe.'

Naomi was right about the men. They jeered at Ruth because she was a Moabite. They accused her of being a thief and a

Each day, the men from Bethlehem gathered in the fields to harvest the corn.

beggar – and worse. Even the steward snorted in disgust when she begged to be allowed to glean.

'Please,' she implored, desperate to find a little barley to take back to the empty house. 'If not for my sake, for my mother-in-law, Naomi.'

The foreman overheard them from his seat high on a camel's back. He frowned at Ruth. 'So you're the Moabite woman who came back with Naomi?'

'Yes.' Ruth's heart was pounding but she looked bravely up at the man.

'Well, what are you doing here?' He pointed into the distance. 'Her land lies over there.'

Ruth tried not to get angry. Surely he knew that Naomi had not been here to plant any seed? 'That land lies barren,' she explained. 'Please let me glean here.'

'I can't give you permission. This land belongs to Boaz.'

'Then let me glean till he arrives! Believe me, I'll not keep a single grain without his consent.'

The foreman thought for a moment. 'Oh, all right. But keep well back from the others. They won't want you joining them.'

'The Lord God bless you,' said Ruth. Suddenly she felt very glad that she had taken the God of the Jews for her own. She felt sure He would protect her. As a child in Moab she had been taught to worship many gods, but she had never felt that they cared for her at all.

As the sun rose high in the sky, Boaz came to see how the work was progressing. His eye was caught by a lone figure still gleaning, although everyone else had retired to the shade for their midday meal. He shaded his eyes to see the young woman better. As she stooped to pick up a single grain, his heart ached with pity.

The foreman came forward to explain his agreement with

Ruth. 'She's a hard worker,' he added. 'She hasn't stopped all morning.'

Boaz poured a drink of water from one of his pitchers and took the cup out into the field to Ruth.

'Here,' he said, offering it to her. 'You must be thirsty.'

Ruth turned bewildered eyes on Boaz. 'My lord, why do you show me such kindness?'

'Because I have heard all that you have done for Naomi. You deserve a rich reward.' He handed her the cup which she took gratefully. The sun was hot and she had not dared stop work to go to the well.

'All I can do', he continued, 'is give you permission to glean wherever you like.'

Ruth lowered her eyes. 'You are most generous.'

Boaz looked thoughtfully at the modest young woman. 'Ruth,' he said at last. 'Work only on my land so that I can make sure that no man troubles you.'

Then he led her off to eat with his dumbfounded workers. When they gave her bread, Boaz noticed that she saved some for Naomi.

Before he left, he took one of his men aside. 'Take some ears from the pile of grain,' he said softly, 'and drop them in her path.'

It was well after dark when Ruth arrived home.

Naomi had been dreadfully worried, but she was delighted when she saw how much grain Ruth had brought.

'And there's more!' Ruth laughed, producing the bread. 'He let me share their meal and I saved some for you.'

'He let…who let you?' Naomi demanded.

Ruth lit the fire before she answered. 'His name is Boaz,' she revealed with a smile. 'And he said I could glean for the whole harvest.'

Naomi put her hand to her throat. 'The Lord God guided you to Boaz, I am certain of it. He owns many fields. And he's a close kinsman of ours. A cousin of my dead husband! May the Lord God bless him for his kindness.'

As Naomi put away the barley she thought about Boaz. Although she knew he was both wise and fair, she had never known him show such kindness to a stranger before....

Every day, Ruth toiled under the hot sun until all the barley had been safely gathered in, and then all through the wheat harvest, too. As the weeks passed, Boaz noticed how hard Ruth worked for her mother-in-law. He admired her very much.

Naomi was full of admiration for Ruth, too. How would she have managed if Ruth had stayed behind? Oh, if only she could do something for Ruth in return. Something that would make Ruth happy for the rest of her life....

By the end of the harvest, Ruth had brought home a vast amount of grain. Naomi was puzzled. How could anyone gather so much just from gleaning? Boaz was good to his men, but surely he would not let them be so careless as to drop this much? Perhaps he had wanted to ensure that the two women did not go hungry, but in that case why did he not simply give them some food? It did not make sense. Unless, perhaps, he had a special reason for wanting Ruth to work near him all day.

When Ruth came home after her last day in the fields she chattered happily about finding fresh work now that the harvest was over.

'You won't find many employers as generous as Boaz,' Naomi remarked.

'No, I'll miss...', then to Naomi's surprise, Ruth cut the sentence short 'I'll miss working on his land,' she mumbled at last. But she would not meet Naomi's eye when she said it, and

although the light was not very good in the house, Naomi was certain that Ruth was blushing.

Naomi urged Ruth to speak to Boaz that night.

Naomi's mind raced. Now she came to think of it, Ruth often looked away when she spoke of Boaz.

The door rattled on its hinges.

'There's a good breeze tonight,' Naomi said thoughtfully – the wind helped the winnowers by blowing the dust and chaff from the grain. 'Boaz will be winnowing long after nightfall again…. So he'll eat and sleep outdoors.' She met her daughter-in-law's eye. 'Ruth, you must speak with him tonight, alone.'

'Why?'

'He's a relation of ours,' Naomi explained. Indeed, Boaz was close enough in law to be considered next-of-kin, close enough to take a brother's place. 'Ruth, if you would only ask him, I know he would honour his duty by marrying you.'

'Marry me?' Ruth could hardly get the words out, her mouth was so dry. 'But I'm a foreigner and a widow.'

Naomi saw pride flash across Ruth's face and knew that Ruth would never ask Boaz. She was convinced he would not want her.

Naomi prayed the Lord God's forgiveness for her next words. 'If you were to have a child together...' she said, knowing full well that Ruth would do anything for her mother-in-law, 'our family name would be restored.'

Ruth could hardly breathe. What was Naomi saying? That it was her duty to ask Boaz to marry her for Naomi's sake, so that the family name would not die out? Her hands began to tremble. 'Tell me what I must do,' she breathed.

'First,' said Naomi briskly, 'we must prepare you.' She brought water for Ruth to wash, and began to anoint Ruth's hair with perfumed oil.

'No one must see you together,' she said. 'Wait until everyone is asleep, then go and lie near him. Uncover his feet. He'll wake later with the cold and...well, he will tell you what to do.'

Ruth was shivering with a mixture of fear and excitement as she hurried through the night to the fields. She knew Boaz would turn her down – she was only going for Naomi's sake – *but what if he said yes?*

Hidden by the darkness, she watched Boaz sitting silently by the fire while his men celebrated the harvest with music and

laughter. At last everyone lay down to sleep. Boaz lay alone beside one of the mounds of grain. Ruth waited until she was certain that everybody was asleep, then she tiptoed out from her hiding-place. She was quaking with fear as she drew back the covering from his feet.

She lay on the hard earth, frightened that he would not wake. But Naomi, as ever, was right. In the chill of the night Boaz did stir, and as he awakened he became aware that someone was at his feet.

'Who are you?' he asked, peering into the darkness.

'Ruth, my lord.' Panic gripped her, and it took a few moments for her to collect herself. She could hardly bring herself to speak the next words, but at last she found the courage. 'Spread the corner of your garment over me,' she whispered, 'for you are my next of kin.'

Boaz sat frozen in the darkness. Could this really be happening? Could Ruth, the young woman who had impressed the whole of Bethlehem with her loyalty and her courage, could she really be asking *him* to do this for her? And then with a jolt of dismay he realized that she had only asked him for Naomi's sake – not because she loved him. 'May God reward you,' he said. 'Such a sacrifice for Naomi's sake is great indeed.' He swallowed. 'You have earned the respect of many. You could have married for love.'

Ruth almost blurted out that she did indeed love him, but she was afraid he would laugh at her.

'Anyway, I am not free to marry you,' Boaz continued gently. 'There is another kinsman, closer in line.' According to the laws of Judea this man had the right to marry Ruth if he chose. 'He must give his consent before I can do what you ask…. But we must wait until morning.'

When dawn broke, he woke her and urged her to go before

anyone saw them together. He gave her barley for Naomi. 'Reassure her that the matter will be settled with honour,' he said. 'Whatever the outcome, you will have a husband today.'

Ruth's eyes smarted as she stumbled back to Bethlehem. How she wished she had never gone! By the end of the day she could be married to some man whom she had never even met!

'Why didn't you tell me we had another kinsman closer in line!' she reproached as Naomi came forward to greet her.

'There is no kinsman more worthy than Boaz!' Naomi insisted.

'He is certainly a man of great honour,' said Ruth.

Naomi patted her comfortingly on the shoulder. 'Boaz is as wise as he is good,' she consoled. 'He will not let another man make you his bride.'

Ruth sighed. How could Boaz marry her if the law said she should marry another man? She did not understand.

But Naomi understood. She knew that while laws must not be broken, sometimes they can be bent.

Boaz was trying to think of a way to bend the law, but he could not. He knew that the moment he told his kinsman that he wanted Ruth for himself, then he would lose her. The man was greedy. If he thought something was valuable he snatched it.

As Boaz walked to the city gates of Bethlehem he racked his brains. He had to settle this matter honourably, but how could he be honourable and still ensure that he became Ruth's husband?

As soon as his kinsman came by, he called him over. 'We have something to discuss,' he said.

Boaz studied the crowd of curious people which began to gather around him, and was pleased to see that there were a number of elders present who would be able to bear witness to his proposal. But then his gaze fell on Ruth and Naomi, standing together a little way off, and his heart began to thud. What if he failed? What if the elders ended up bearing witness to the marriage of Ruth and his greedy kinsman? He could hardly bear to think of it.

He took a deep breath and turned to his kinsman. 'You are of Elimelech's clan, like me,' he said firmly. 'Now, his widow, Naomi, has put her land up for sale. If you wish to buy the land, and honour the obligations which accompany it, tell us now. If

Boaz told his kinsman that Naomi's land was up for sale.

you do not, I myself will buy it since I am next in line after you.'

The kinsman's eyes lit up when Boaz mentioned that he would like the land. 'I will buy it,' the man said quickly.

'You do realize', continued Boaz carefully, 'that on the day you buy the land you also buy Ruth, the widow of Elimelech's elder son? You must do this in order to revive the family name.' He deliberately did not say that he wanted Ruth himself.

The kinsman frowned. Land…. Yes, he wanted the land that Boaz was so keen on…. But some widow for a wife? That was another matter.

'You'll have children,' warned a bystander. 'And they'll have first claim on the land, not you.'

'And on your other property, no doubt,' muttered someone else.

The kinsman was alarmed. 'Then I cannot. Boaz, take my right yourself,' he insisted. Quickly, he dragged off his shoe and thrust it into Boaz' hand – an old tradition which indicated that a deal had been struck. 'Before the elders here, I recognize your right to walk upon our kinswoman's land,' he proclaimed.

Boaz gripped the shoe so hard that his knuckles blanched. He waved it above his head. 'You are witnesses that I now buy from Naomi everything which belonged to Elimelech. Also I…' He hesitated. He was not *buying* Ruth…he did not want anyone to think that his future wife

Boaz held up the shoe and the agreement was sealed.

could be bought and sold! 'Also,' he continued,' Ruth the Moabitess, I take as my wife!'

From out of the crowd came a cry. Boaz saw Ruth looking at him with wide eyes. Had she cried out in dismay? Did she not want him? His heart sank.

Boaz did not see Ruth again until the sun was setting and she was brought to his house dressed in her wedding finery. As she walked towards him she kept her eyes cast down. It tore at his heart that she would not look at him, but at last she did look up. She looked right into his eyes – and he saw her love for him burning there as unmistakeably as it had burned on the day she had taken Naomi's people for her own. And when Boaz offered her his hand, she took it so eagerly that any last doubts melted away.

When the spring harvest came again, Ruth became a mother. She laid the newborn baby in Naomi's arms.

'You have a son once more,' she said gently.

The baby blinked at the light; his little hands waved in the air as he reached for his grandmother. Naomi's

Naomi took
Ruth's child,
Obed, in her
arms.

eyes filled with tears of happiness.

All the neighbours came in. These days they loved Ruth almost as much as Naomi did. They crowded round the baby.

'May the Lord God bless him,' they said. One of them begged her to call him Obed.

Naomi smiled down at Ruth's child. 'Obed!' she said. 'The servant of the Lord.'

And indeed Obed did serve the Lord, because when he grew up he became the father of Jesse, and Jesse became the father of David, and David became King of all Israel.

TESTAMENT

THE ANIMATED BIBLE

Adapted by Sally Humble-Jackson

BOXTREE **S4C**

STORIES FROM THE OLD TESTAMENT

available from Boxtree

CREATION AND THE FLOOD

God warns Noah that He will send a great flood to punish
the wickedness of mankind, but tells him to build an ark
and bring into it two of every animal to begin a new
life. As he and his family huddle among the animals in
the dark belly of the huge ark, Noah tells them the story
of God's creation of the earth, and of Adam and Eve, as
the flood waters destroy the world outside.

£4.99

ISBN: 0 7522 1023 8

MOSES

Murder, escape, visions, plagues and the parting of the
Red Sea: all these form the spectacular drama of the
Israelite exodus from Egypt. But this is also the story
of one man's journey from hotheaded youth to a man who
becomes the mouthpiece of God – Moses.

£4.99

ISBN: 0 7522 1003 3

RUTH

One of the oldest love stories and one of the most beautiful, appealing heroines. When her mother-in-law Naomi loses everything in Moab, the widow Ruth journeys with her back to Bethlehem where her loyalty, forbearance and selflessness is rewarded by a God who cares for the poor and broken.

£4.99

ISBN: 0 7522 1008 4

ELIJAH

The story of one man pitted against a kingdom that has betrayed God. Elijah arranges a contest between God and the prophets of Baal; the prophets are vanquished but Queen Jezebel maintains her vendetta against him. Elijah flees into the desert where he meets God in an unforgettable encounter.

£4.99

ISBN: 0 7522 1013 0